HOME ALONE

COLORING BOOK

THIS BOOK BELONGS TO

____

____

TEST COLOR PAGE

"I made my family
DISAPPEAR!"

STAY AT HOME.
YA FILTHY ANIMALS

PROTECT THE NHS

HOME ALONE™

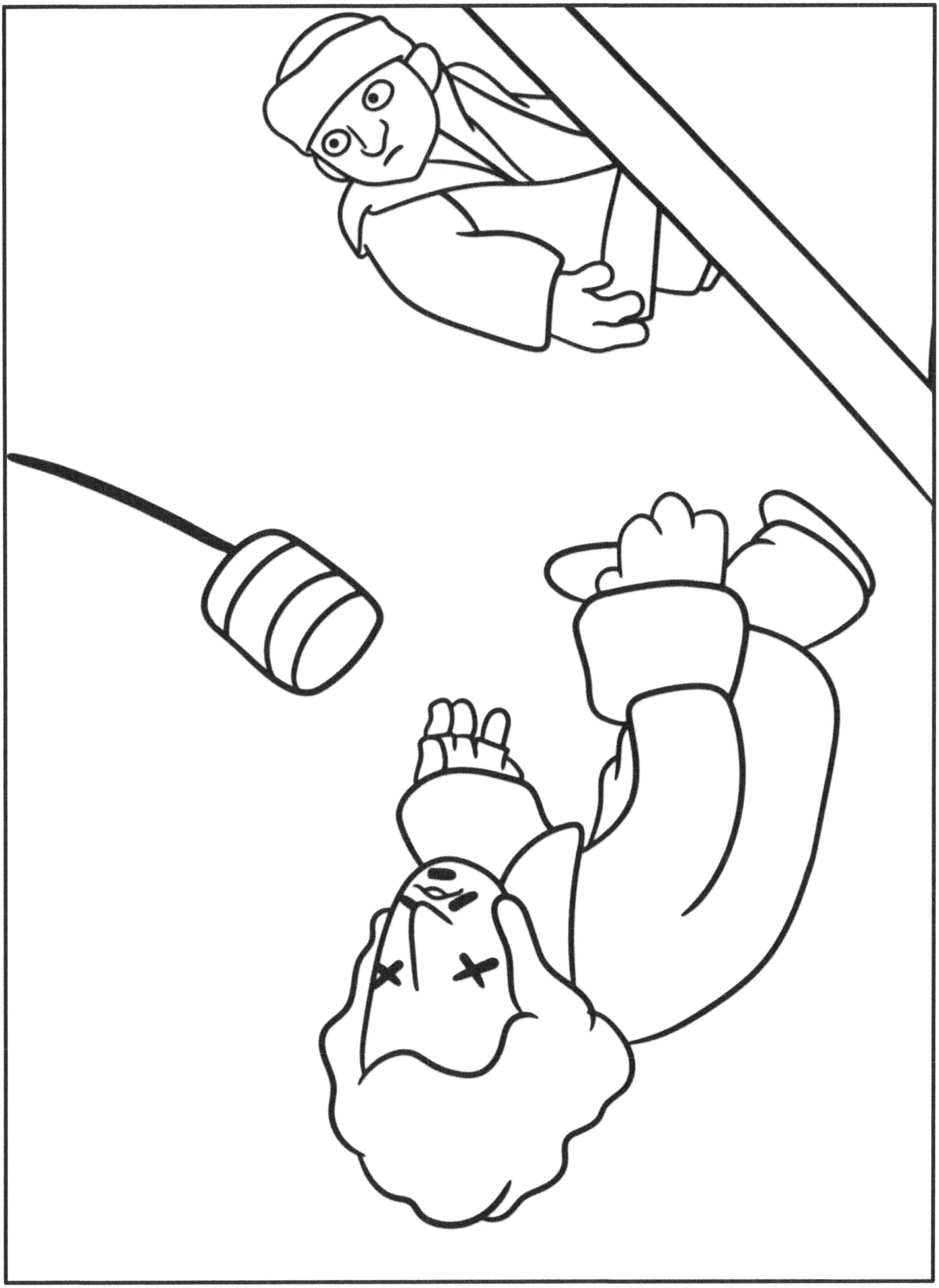

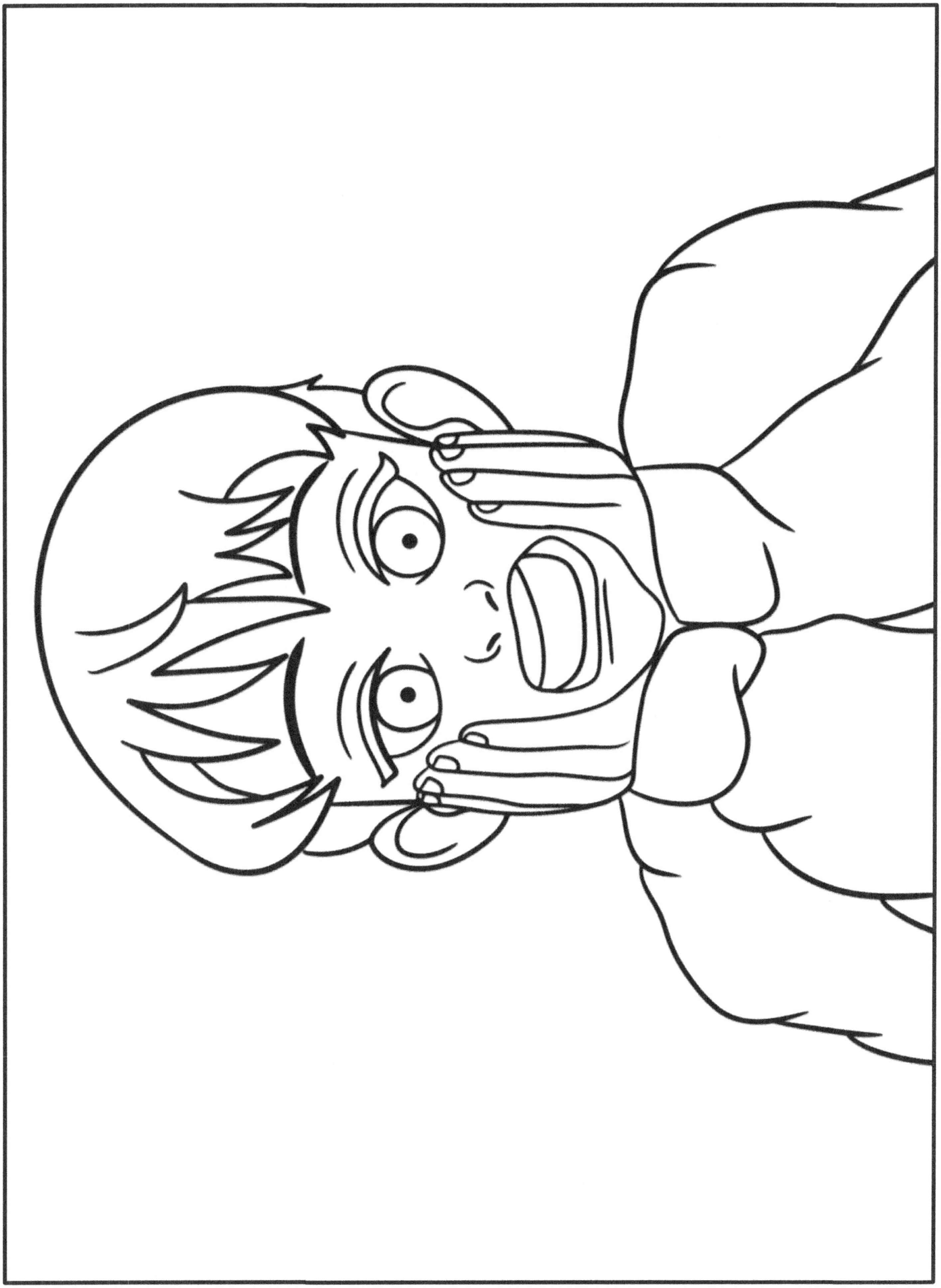

"I AIN'T GOING IN THERE."
"ME NEITHER."

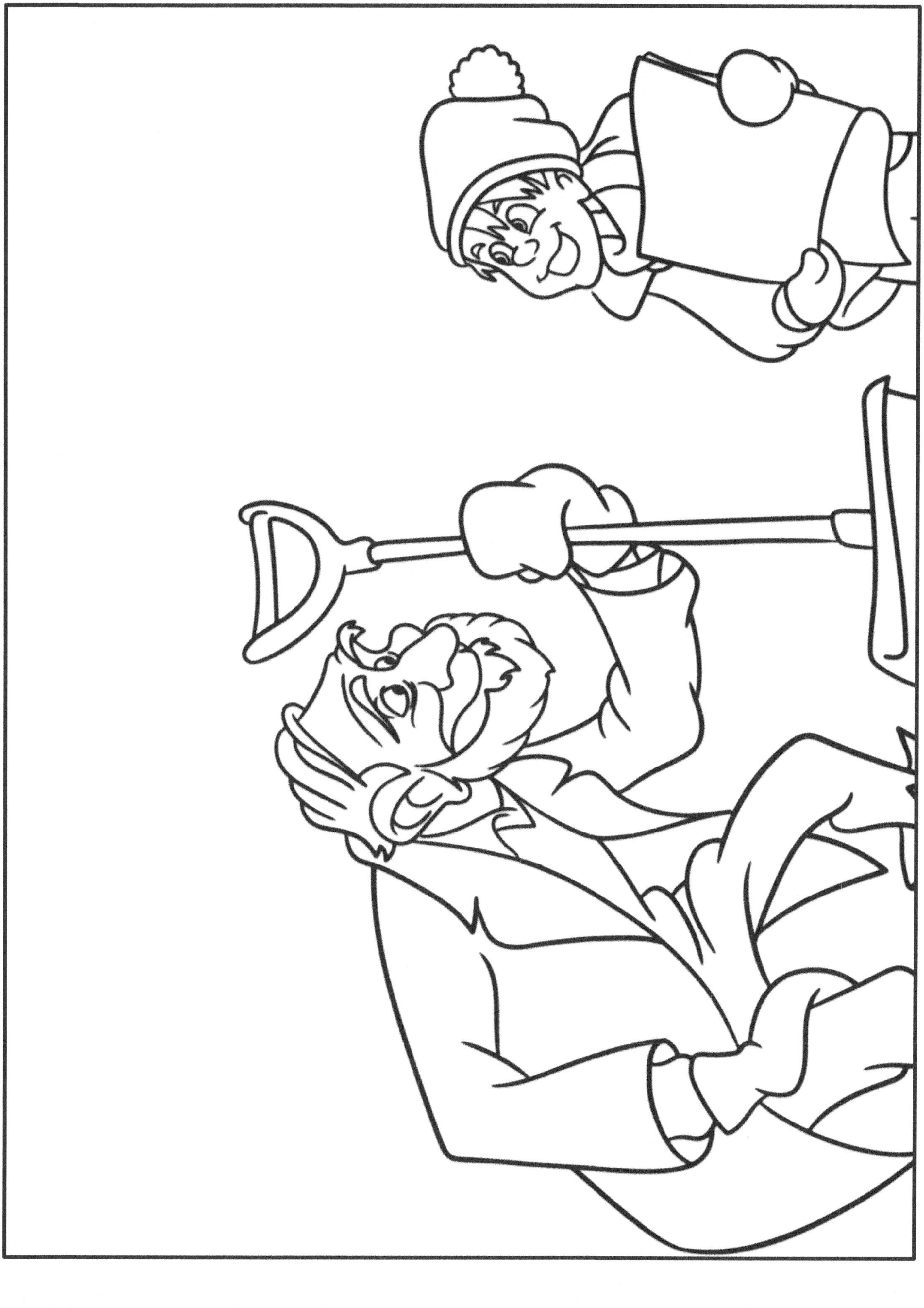

Made in the USA
Monee, IL
15 January 2023

25352838R00039